COMING HOME

COMING HOME

Modern Rustic

Creative Living in Dutch Interiors

by Barbara de Vries

foreword by Lidewij Edelkoort

RIZZOLI
NEW YORK

New York · Paris · London · Milan

TABLE OF CONTENTS

6
STAIRWAY TO HEAVEN
by Lidewij Edelkoort

11
GOING DUTCH
by Barbara de Vries

19
MAKING SPACE INTO PLACE

37
DANCING ON WATER

51
LISTENING TO THE DUNES

67
LAMBS IN THE CITY

83
SPINNING WOOL INTO GOLD

95
I AM WHAT I MAKE

113
LOVE ON THE MAAS

131
REINVENTING THE PAST

151
BALANCING THE FUTURE

161
LIVE, WORK, CREATE

179
WASTE NOTHING

191
THE STATION MASTERS

207
LIVING IN NATURE

221
VAN GOGH'S NEIGHBORS

238
ACKNOWLEDGMENTS

Flying into Schiphol airport, it becomes clear how much of my country has been designed into a neat green and khaki patchwork of little allotments, twinkling streams and major canals, that are punctuated by bright white sails and reflected by monumental glass greenhouses, which feed and flower not just this little nation, but large parts of the world. It is a rigorous pattern that could've been painted by Piet Mondrian, providing the colors were changed to primaries. (Piet hated green and is known to have painted the stem of a tulip white, to escape the terror of this color.)

I left Holland in my early twenties, to live and work in Paris, pursuing a career as a forecaster of cultural change and future scenarios. I visit my country at erratic intervals, and each return is emotional and colored with mild melancholia.

Flying back over my homeland, I smile in recognition of the skills of this country's people. Early in the seventeenth century, they set sail to the other side of the planet and brought back tulips from Turkey, licorice from Egypt, potatoes from Peru, and carpets from Persia. They even bartered the Isle of Manhattan for a tiny island that specialized in nutmeg. These Dutchmen were flying high on spices, flowers, and textiles and built their great cities nutmeg by nutmeg, from only small consumption goods that they traded as if they were gold. Even today, this spirit of trade in the humble and ordinary perseveres. Rooted in basic, functional beauty it is palpable in the success of Dutch design. The country's agricultural roots still come through in the crafting of cups, vases, bowls, long tables, functional chairs, and clever cabinets. This specifically Dutch design language seems to thrive during culturally difficult times and has been an ongoing international success since the world dramatically changed on 2001, 2008, and 2020.

In the Lowlands of the Netherlands, people are acutely conscious of the fact that they live under sea level and can only exist because of the major water-works protecting their land. Having one common enemy, namely the terrifying forces of water, has shielded the country from being torn apart by ideological and theological disputes, which might otherwise have led to damaging schisms and skirmishes. But not so in this doll-sized promised land. Often, the mindset is naive, as when the Dutch army went out to fight the Germans on their bicycles. This image always endears me to these insouciant people who don't seem to acknowl-edge other agendas, as if unaware of danger. Although the country has flaws and is behind on a much-needed reckoning with their part in the history of the African slave trade, the Dutch generally have a strong sense of goodwill and accountability. People are in control of their lives since they have designed their destinies. They are instinctively creative and resourceful. With feet firmly positioned in a flat clay landscape and the brain immersed in formidable cloudscapes, being Dutch is like being a conduit, directly connecting fantasy with reality. The result is sparkling and sparse at the same time; a unique mix of Protestant pragmatism mixed with fantastic bolds of illumination.

Making do with what one has been given as ingredients, money and talent are the creative currency of the Dutch culture and shapes people to become entrepreneurial and self-reliable. We are fed on higher goals with the power of self as as our daily porridge, creative thinking as our bread and butter, and intuition as the ultimate ingredient. This regimen creates people that cherish jam as a delicious gift.

In this book, writer and photographer Barbara de Vries, who left the Netherlands when she was eighteen, analyzes the lives and styles of several of our compatriots, all different in age, location, and work, yet all united in talent and taste. Their houses could be our houses, their design solutions each other's solutions. To illustrate this point, Barbara includes images of her own homestead in Pennsylvania, in recognition of the kinship we all share. They represent what is best in the prolific country garden pretending to be a country, where cities still resemble villages, with neighborhoods remembering their origins, and citizens reinventing what life in the twenty-first century is destined to become. Her subjects harness their talents, they safeguard their families and they share their work, which feels more like play than anything else. They freewheel through life as conscientious citizens, paying attention to each other and their land—while working to reverse damage done in former centuries. They bicycle with their kids to discover flowers, to harvest mushrooms and to get exercise without noticing. In these houses there are no gyms. Focused on places to work and experiment, the kitchen comes first and then the atelier, the studio, and the arts and crafts spaces. Styles are amalgamated: contemporary furniture with old fashioned couches, textiles, colors, and outsider art. These are hybrid homes where the young and old as well as the new and old blend into one beautiful bric-a-brac. There's no minimalism in sight as the author's eye picks up on fully filled cupboards with diverse ceramics, stunning collections of photography, textiles, and objects that speak in local dialects. Meals are shared, cakes baked, and fires stoked while friends and family gather. Kids come and go and make a mess. We call this the household of Jan Steen, after his famous painting in which even dogs and babies share in the messy merriness of the moment.

What all these spaces have in common, and what has been perfectly captured by Barbara's lens, are the staircases of the different houses. Even the boat has cute steps to sit on! But why is the staircase so prominent in Dutch architecture? Could it be that the Dutch reach toward the sky because they endeavor to make the most of limited space using cellars for preserving fruits, attics for ateliers, and barns for celebration? Sometimes redesigned, often restored and even recycled, stairs and ladders share the same linear, elevating principle: guiding the eye to higher goals, a tool for ascension to elevated awareness. Painted in lovely colors and finished with warm waxes, these staircases are indeed like Led Zeppelin's song "Stairway to Heaven," expressing old ideas of faith and fortune, while guiding us into the realm of hope and dreams.

Lidewij Edelkoort, Paris, 2020

Our Dutch windmill, the *Molen*, was my father's wedding gift to my mother. When he died, not long after the renovation of his dream home was complete, I complemented the scant memories I had of him with memories of all the summers spent at our *molen*. It was the place where I felt free to create my own universe while I imagined him there, my architect father, romantic, inventive, and hopeful, building a new world for my mother and me.

Coming Home is a peek inside the homes of fourteen couples and individuals, who live thoughtful, creative lives in reclaimed environments of their own making. I have tried to capture the meaning of *gezellig*, a unique word that's at the heart of being Dutch and almost impossible to describe in English. If it were a recipe, the ingredients would be equal parts of happy, cozy, fun, and belonging.

I reconnected to being Dutch when Kiki and Leila, my twin daughters, started college in the Netherlands. The houses and lives featured on these pages are an evolution of where I left off when I moved from Amsterdam to London to study fashion design. To me, these homes and lives characterize the best of Dutch living.

Without going deep into our national history, it's fair to say that we are a single minded, outspoken, righteous, and practical people, who constantly contradict themselves by being cozy, cute, open minded, and irreverent. We even bewilder ourselves as we defend Dutch traditions while rebelling against them at the same time, a trait that was drilled into us by our parents with the old Dutch adage: "Oh please, do act normal! When you act normal you're crazy enough."

This kind of crazy can be found in the homes and lives featured here, from a chair wearing a jacket and baby lambs leaping around a historic house, to an outdoor bathtub on a barge, and a chandelier made from Chinese soupspoons.

Converted Dutch buildings like farms, barns, and garages may look conventional from the outside, but often embody complete anarchy on the inside, the good kind of anarchy, where the rules are challenged to find new, more sustainable ways of living.

The homes in this book have been transformed into laboratories for modern lives. Most of the people work from home, which was further encouraged by the Covid-19 pandemic. Many admitted that the lockdowns didn't really impact the way they lived, but it did make them more creative and productive as they explored the "new normal."

In this small, overpopulated country, the effects of overconsumption, waste, and carbon footprint are on everyone's mind and inspire reusing and recycling materials rather than buying new. For instance, Rolf Bruggink (see "Waste Nothing," pages 179-89) bought two adjacent buildings: a historic coach house and an abandoned barrack from the 1950s. He demolished the barrack and used all its salvage to create the interior of the coach house.

While the Dutch are notoriously money conscious and thrifty, another contradiction lies in their natural sense of social justice. Those who think that capitalism and socialism cannot coexist need to look no further than the Netherlands, where altruism is as normal as riding a bike. There are no medals bestowed or red carpets rolled out for those who give back. In fact, public displays of "virtue signaling" are perceived as an embarrassment of riches.

I too contradict my Dutch self by making this book. At age eighteen, I saw a bright future everywhere but in the Netherlands and after I left Amsterdam, I did not look back. Instead, I lived in Paris and Australia, before settling in London to study fashion design. I'd made my own clothes since I was twelve, then made clothes for my friends, and eventually sold them at local boutiques before I'd even graduated from high school. When I came across the work of French/Japanese designer Kenzo, I realized that being a fashion designer could actually be a career, one that happened in places like Paris, London, and Milan. I entered that world as a fashion model, earning the tuition money I needed for studying in London. Along the way, I shaped my life with friends, boyfriends, homes, and eventually my own fashion company in London. In the late 1980s, I moved to New York, where I became Director of Design at Calvin Klein and created the CK collections. I got married, had three daughters, built two country homes, started more design companies, and was never homesick once.

Only when I moved to Miami in 2009 did I begin to relate to the new wave of cutting-edge designers from the Netherlands, who were showcased at Art Basel/ Design Miami. Around the same time, the Dutch consulate featured my work with recycled beach plastic (pollution) in some of their presentations. They gave me an award for my "contribution to the environment" and I worked with them on local education programs. Once again, I was speaking my native language daily. It took living in Florida for nine years, for me to feel Dutch again!

My twins were in their final year of high school when we visited Amsterdam to celebrate my mother's ninetieth birthday. When they began fantasizing about studying in the Netherlands, I started seeing my birth country through their eyes. It was cozy. It was small. It felt safe. Teenagers seemed independent as they rode their bikes everywhere. My mother was funny and her home *gezellig*, and they discovered that they had an extended family of aunts, uncles, and several cute cousins their own age.

A few months later we drove around the Netherlands, visiting colleges. We reveled in the landscape, from quaint villages and historic inner cities to fields of tulips and modern wind turbines. We rented bicycles, drank endless mint teas, ate *poffertjes*, fries with mayo, and I made them try raw herring and Indonesian food. I showed them where I used to live, went to school, had my first kiss, and bought my fabrics. I taught them how to use the bike paths, trains, and trams, and how to say *dankjewel*, *gezellig*, and *lekker*. Not only did I see Dutch life in the twenty-first century through my daughters' eyes but I also relived my own childhood. In a sense, I "came home."

My father was an architect who, after the devastation of WWII, specialized in social housing, and my mother was a photographer. Consequently, I became a very visual person and I treated fashion design as architecture for the body. My early collections were inspired by London street style of the 1980s, and when I joined Calvin Klein in the 1990s, professional young New Yorkers became a source of inspiration. When we moved to Miami, I took a break from fashion. Instead Alastair, my husband, and I began publishing illustrated books and I returned to my heritage of photography and architecture.

Life came full circle when I realized that the way we live in the United States was not so different from the lives and homes featured in this book. Our Pennsylvania homestead, a 1790 farmhouse that I bought soon after coming to New York, is very *gezellig*. We too mix the old, new, and quirky found objects with heirlooms, art, and lots of books. We make art, grow food, and live thoughtfully in nature. As our family expanded we built a modern addition, and we run the publishing company from our studios there. Our lives are an open book, as we share our home with family, friends, colleagues, and neighbors.

I am grateful for the Dutch spirit of "having nothing to hide." The ease with which people reveal their lives is perhaps best expressed by the absence of curtains in most Dutch houses. As a child, peeking into the homes in my neighborhood, inspired dreams of my future. There was one place where a black cat always stared back at me from a simple white room with only a sewing machine on the dining table and a tailor's dummy in the corner. At home, our large live-in kitchen was level with the street. It had three big windows with deep windowsills where the milkman left our milk and yogurt. Neighbors would walk by and wave at us. Sometimes my mother would open the window and chat with a passing friend. My sister and I would play right outside, our mom watching us as she cooked. For us, the lack of curtains meant a sense of connection to our neighborhood, until a flasher was seen roaming our street and the vintage red-striped curtains came out of storage. For several months we hid from the outside world and that was cozy too.

Barbara de Vries, Milford, 2020

Making space into place is how designers Ina Meijer and Matt van Cruijsen describe their life. This somehow makes sense as I'm trying to find their place in the vast open spaces of Friesland. It feels like the horizon is lower than anywhere else, as if there's more sky and light. The endless green polders, as flat as the sea, are outlined by a grid of narrow canals like a Mondrian painting. The pastures are dotted with cows, sheep, Friesian horses and thatched farmhouses. Vast modern barns and bright yellow farm equipment are evidence that the land is still being worked. Shortly after driving through the village of Pingjum I spot a red mailbox with INAMATT printed in white letters. There's a traditional Friesian farmhouse to the left and several barns to the right.

"That farmhouse first brought us here, twelve years ago," Matt says, as he helps me unload my camera equipment from the car. He goes on to explain that a friend, a well-known Dutch film director, hired them to renovate and design its interior. "We loved working here—the light and space," Ina adds, "so when these two barns came on the market, we snapped them up."

They began by converting the cow barn, putting a concrete floor in the old stables and creating open-plan areas for living, cooking, eating, and working. The original windows were small, so they brought in more light by replacing the barn doors with large panels of glass and adding bay windows. The hayloft became the second floor, with two bedrooms, a claw foot tub, and a separate bathroom. "Our home is our design lab," Ina says, "and we like blurring the boundaries between life and work."

Throughout the barn, they created quirky tableaux that combine their own work with found objects, like the vintage chair that wears a linen button-back jacket, a design they first developed for the guest rooms of the Exchange Hotel in Amsterdam.

We drink green tea and eat homemade hummus from the cups and plates that they designed for a Japanese tea ceremony, which included everything from the porcelain tea service to candy and table linens, even the kimono. "We love working in Japan, and we're doing a Google launch in Tokyo, next month," Ina says. Most of their work seems incongruous with the austere Dutch farmland that surrounds us, but they don't feel out of place. "Sure, it's quiet," Matt says, "but when you're faced with yourself it can only lead to being more creative and making better work." Ina adds that Amsterdam is just an hour away, and that they often go into the city for meetings and dinner with friends. "We're always happy to come back here at night," she says.

I'm about to ask about their involvement in the local community, when the phone rings. Matt answers and the shrill voice of a young boy explains that he has to cancel his visit that afternoon. He sounds disappointed, almost in tears, but his mother can't drive him over today. Matt is kind and promises there will be plenty more opportunities and that the weather isn't very nice anyway. The boy

seems reluctant to let go. Perhaps he hopes that someone will offer to fetch him, but after several goodbyes they finally hang up. "We have a group of local kids who come and make art with us," Ina says. Matt goes on to show me how they created a new font that was painted by "studio babies," the children of friends and neighbors. "We covered the wall with a large sheet of white paper and gave them paint rollers and black paint," Matt says. "Then they painted the entire alphabet." They used these letters for the branding of Pickle de Winkel, a "no waste" food concept, on everything from the jars, bottles, and flyers to the store window and website.

Another barn, which had been used for storing farm equipment, was turned into Ina's textile studio. Now, a decade later, they've just finished building a third barn and find themselves spending more time there. "Extra space creates a shift within yourself and we always end up living where we work," Ina says.

The third barn allows them a new level of collaboration with their clients, like the designers from G-Star, the well-known Dutch Jeans brand, who arrived earlier in the day. They worked with the INAMATT team all morning, had lunch at the long farm table, and returned to Amsterdam in the afternoon. "Without office interruptions, this space becomes a world our clients can step into and create a new universe," Matt says.

Ina and Matt employ about fifteen people, who work four days a week. This gives the younger team members a chance to stay connected to their life in the city, while others have moved up to Friesland, where real estate is still affordable, and started families in and around Pingjum.

A few years back, Ina and Matt bought the red brick cottage to the right of the new barn. It's become a home away from home, where team members who live in the city can spend the night. Siep, the original farmer of all the land that surrounds them, had retired to this cottage after his family moved away. Lore has it that, on weekends, old Siep would sit at the end of his driveway and sell his potatoes to anyone who passed by. Apparently, he didn't need to do it to make money; he did it to stay in touch with the locals who'd stop and chat and buy his produce.

"We now try to come up with similar ideas that keep us equally connected to the community," Matt says.

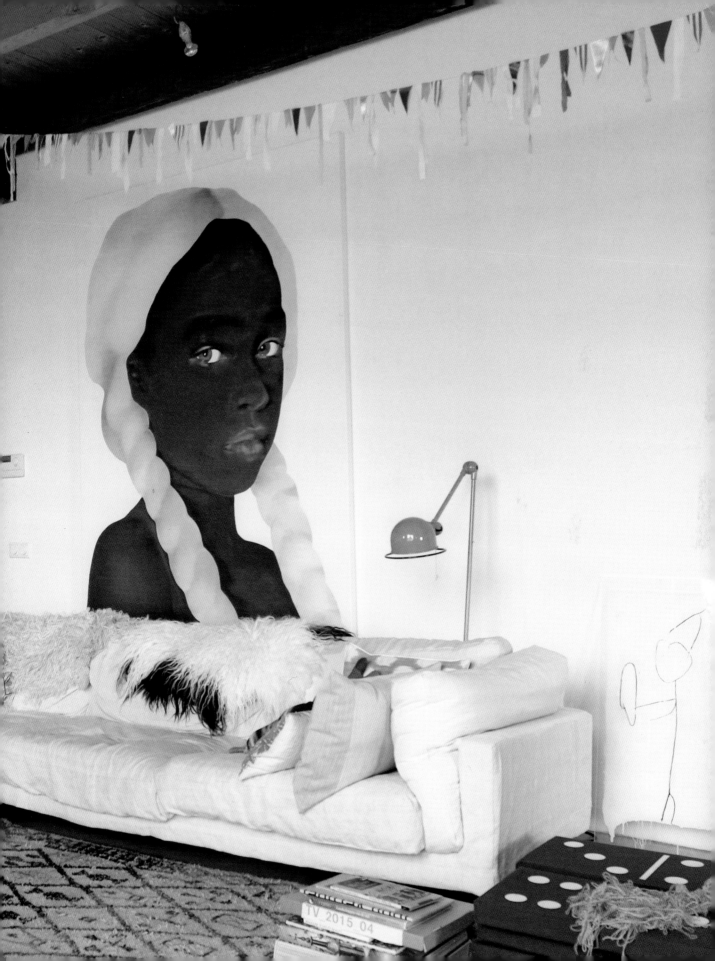

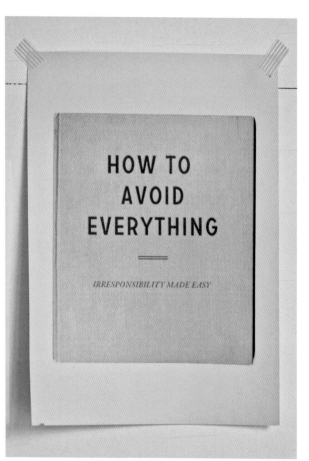

HOW TO
AVOID
EVERYTHING

IRRESPONSIBILITY MADE EASY

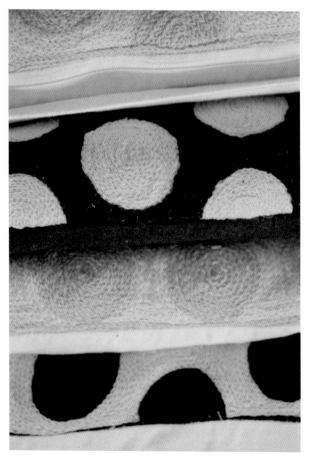

There are three thousand houseboats moored in and around Amsterdam, yet I do not have a single childhood memory of visiting one. I fantasized about them though, riding my bicycle along the canals, and picking the coziest out of the different design styles, which ranged from modern floating boxes to old cargo barges, all decorated in personal colors, with walls of glass and terraces with potted flowers, trees, hammocks, cats, dogs, and even garden gnomes. So, I'm especially excited to visit Laura de Monchy and John Hannema, whose converted barge is moored somewhere on the IJ, Amsterdam's historic harbor.

The large barges are neatly stacked alongside each other. There are dozens of them. I worry that I won't be able to find Laura's, they're all so similar and, unlike the row of brand-new townhouses across the street, they don't seem to have numbers. I walk back and forth several times before I pull up the scouting pictures on my phone and match them to one of the larger ships. Tentatively, I weave my way past a bench, kids' bikes, and potted plants and cross the gangway onto the ship. To the right is a small skipper's cabin and to the left must be the living space. Everything feels different from entering a house: the scale, sounds, and the unsteady floor beneath my feet. A neatly stacked pile of firewood next to the front door seems out of place yet comforting.

"I bought my first boat when I was twenty," Laura tells me. She's tall, radiant and seems more interested in asking about my life than being interviewed. "I had a small inheritance from my parents," she explains as she pours me a mug of tea. "I designed these," she adds, lifting the cup above my head to show the detail on its china base—a large yellow bolt. The small barge came with a mooring on Borneo Island, the quays where Dutch ocean liners used to be docked. "The owner didn't like living here," she says. "It was kind of rough with salvage everywhere." But for Laura, then an art student at the Rietveld Academy, the abandoned oil drums, rusting anchors, bollards, and cleats, were a source of inspiration. For her graduate show she collected the empty drums and canisters and cast their shapes in pastel colored porcelain. "My teachers thought I was too wild," she laughs, "but my vases ended up being published everywhere."

Laura met John Hannema in 2006. As a chef and artist, he was known for staging ingenious pop-up dinners in his apartment. "We wanted to live together," Laura says, "but he found my boat too cramped, and I didn't want to live on land." They decided to keep the mooring and buy a bigger ship together. After a long search they found a 130-foot Belgian Spitz barge that was used for hauling freight over European rivers and canals. It had been lovingly maintained by its skipper and only ever carried "soft cargo" like grain. "Most old cargo boats are beaten up," Laura says, "but this one was in perfect shape."

Her brother, Joris van Hoytema, is an architect, and the three of them worked on the conversion together. Laura wanted an outdoor bath and big, open spaces. John wanted a pear tree and a great kitchen. Joris wanted to make sure the

cargo hold would be light and airy. He installed skylights, eighteen oversized bronze portholes, and a central patio that would hold John's pear tree and Laura's tub. A year later they moved in, and now they can't imagine living any other way. Borneo Island has since been developed into a real community, with single family houses as well as shops and schools, making it a popular neighborhood. As soon as the weather is good John and Laura have barbecues on their deck and local kids come over to swim in the harbor and warm up in the tub afterward. Over time they've added an extra bedroom for Fosta, their eleven-year-old daughter, as Vonk, her brother, moved into her old room. The old pear tree died recently, and Laura replaced it with a herb garden. "For now," she laughs, "we'll get John another pear tree next spring."

John is the creator of Rijk van de Keizer, a quirky restaurant and popular event space in an old ammunition depot, overlooking typical Dutch farmland on the edge of Amsterdam West. A secluded oasis, it has overgrown gardens full of wildflowers, wicker chairs, tree lanterns, huts and tents, and a colonnade of converted brick warehouses that are filled with long tables and other vintage furniture. Their old Mercedes, cut in half, sits like an eccentric settee overlooking a canal that's accentuated by knot willows. Laura's design influence is everywhere, from recycled lighting fixtures, to blown glass carafes, and my favorite: a salt dish made from an oyster shell perched on the bottom of a broken wineglass. She also maintains the kitchen gardens that supply the restaurant. Together, John and Laura add special touches to weddings, bringing the outside in, like a farm cart filled with black cauliflowers, and dazzling field bouquets in huge old vases.

Laura makes us *tosties* (grilled cheese) for lunch. She tells me how the barge is at the very core of her life, how she loves to find out how its mechanisms work, and how, when things onboard break, she fixes them herself, how this carries over into her design work, and how the craft of making shoes suddenly seemed so elemental. "I went back to school," she says, "because I wanted to be able to make shoes myself." She shows me the wooden lasts for John's and her kids' feet. She is drawn to artisanal design and produces bracelets in Mali. She also works with Return to Sender, a women's empowerment project in the Far East, run by Dutch actress Katja Schuurman. She shows me the new collection of porcelain plates she created in Thailand.

The next day I visit Laura at her studio, in a small warehouse complex not far from her boat. She's sitting on the floor, working on a giant heart-shaped light fixture, threading an electric cord through the frame, while talking of her love for mixing contrasts, and how opposites attract. She stops for a moment and looks at me. "Money is not so important," she says, "with a husband who has a restaurant, there's always good food on the table, and as long as there's enough dancing in the living room, a warm bath and a fire in the stove, we're happy."

Driving to Jetty and Maarten Min's house in Bergen aan Zee is a road well traveled for me. I spent the summers of my childhood in Bergen, at the real Dutch windmill that had been my father's wedding gift to my mother. When the weather was good we'd pack up our towels, shovels, and buckets, and head to the beach in our tiny red Fiat 500.

There's only one street that leads to the sea, and Maarten and Jetty's house is in a row of villas on the left. Their house blends so well with the dunes that I miss the driveway, and I'm forced to continue to the beach access where my mother would drop us off before she looked for a parking spot. I loop back and park in front of the garage that is set into the dune. Maarten awaits me at the top of long, stone steps. Out of breath, I follow him into the house, past a huge tree trunk and up more stairs. "It took us over twenty years to build this place," Maarten says. Jetty greets me on the main floor and offers me an espresso that comes in a white cup with black wings. "As architects, we were always thinking ahead of our last design, never catching up with ourselves," she says.

It's hard to tell where Jetty ends and Maarten begins, and vice versa. They've been working and living together for fifty years, ever since college. Maarten grew up in nearby Bergen, and, after graduating from architecture school, planned to go out in to the world. But Jetty, who was a visual artist, found Maarten's village as well as his bohemian family, irresistible. "When I first walked in, his father was painting at an easel and his mother was playing the ukulele with a child on her lap," she says.

They initially lived in Amsterdam but eventually returned to Bergen and bought an old bar in the center of town. It had lots of small rooms that Jetty filled with bunk beds and rented out to summer tourists. This extra income supported their freelance life as independent architects. "We always worked together, even when I was the one they hired," Maarten says. Becoming partners in their own firm was an organic transition. Maarten, with a traditional education, feels that Jetty, as an artist challenging the establishment, has become the better all-around architect. "The rules can't get around her," he says, "she'll take a template and turn it on itself." Jetty interrupts to praise Maarten's craftsmanship. Listening to them, gives me a sense of how they collaborate fluidly, naturally, and with little conflict.

By 1987, working and living in the same place was taking a toll on their sanity. "Clients dropped by at midnight, often with a bottle of wine, to discuss changes to a plan, and then our employees would arrive at nine the next morning," Maarten says.

Jetty had always dreamed of living near the sea, and suggested moving to Bergen aan Zee, but Maarten wasn't convinced. The village of Bergen had an intellectual year-round community, but the neighboring beach resort was for tourists. When Jetty found a midcentury bungalow in the dunes bordering a nature preserve, they agreed on spending a trial winter there. When, after a few austere months,

spring came, they cherished being close to nature and a year later they bought the property. "We were redesigning the place from day one," Jetty says. "We wanted to build high enough to get views of the sea." The inspiration for the new house came from the way the dunes and local vegetation are shaped by the direction of the wind. With a height of two stories at the neighbors' end and three stories at the other end, the house also appears as if shaped by sea breezes.

They had a hard time finding the right material for the exterior. "We didn't want anything conventional like combinations of wood, brick, and roofing tiles. We were looking for something that would follow the roofline all the way to the ground," Maarten says. The opportunity to create a new material is exactly the kind of challenge that gets Jetty excited. "I'm like an alchemist, who works with elements that can be perceived as boring, but actually allow me to make magic," she says. She was looking for a low maintenance and sustainable material that could work as roofing as well as siding. After a year and a half of research and false starts, she found Petersen Tegl, a Danish brick manufacturer who agreed to help. Together they developed a large ceramic tile that overlaps vertically on the roof but also stacks horizontally to form a wall. They used a special clay that acquires an uneven brownish finish after baking—a natural texture that blends beautifully with the sand, fir trees, and tall grass of the surrounding dunes.

One winter day in 2012, with a snowstorm in the forecast, they went to the unfinished house with trestle tables, mattresses, food, and wine, and camped out. "I needed to feel the house around me; the light throughout the day, the coziest place for sleeping. How I moved around the space," Jetty says, as she stands up and gestures for me to follow her on a tour of the house. We start downstairs, with the bathroom, where the tub appears set in sand, dune grass and fir trees, separated only by floor-to-ceiling glass. "Just the cows occasionally spy on me," she laughs.

The entry hallway is purposely small, and leads into a staircase to the expansive main level. Books are stacked all the way up the steps, creating an extended bookcase.

Arriving at the top is like entering a cathedral. The soaring roof is supported by huge tree trunks and arched beams accentuate the curve of the vaulted ceiling. As the kitchen appears in front of me, I expect the living room to be on the other end, but the sofa seems to be more like a large bed. In fact it looks as if twin couches are pushed together, facing each other, and covered with a linen comforter. Two identical built-in desks sit at either end. "When we camped out, we realized this was the coziest corner of the house, and since it's just the two of us we can sleep wherever we like," Jetty says, waving her hand toward the adjacent 13,000-acre dune preserve.

"I wanted real trees," Jetty says, rubbing the bark of a massive tree trunk that reaches from the ground floor to the roof. After working with an engineer on load-bearing calculations, she found a Dutch tree farm near the German border

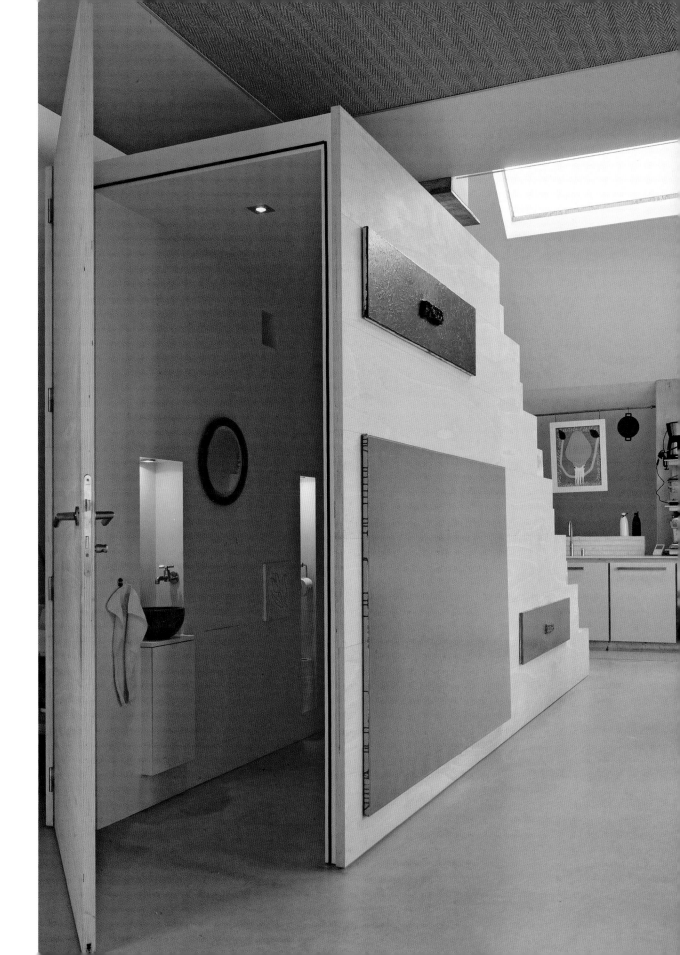

that grew strong, tall, and straight Douglas firs. She selected ten of them. Each one had to be cut and carefully processed by hand to keep their bark intact, before they were dispatched to Bergen. Jetty admits that getting the huge trunks up the steep hill, and in position was quite an ordeal. "In the process I got to know each tree, and I carefully picked their place around the perimeter of the house," she says. "It was like seating guests at a dinner party."

The last stage included hanging the collection of Dutch expressionist paintings by Jaap Min, Maarten's father, and finding a place for the steel cabinet by Piet Hein Eek that Jetty filled with her rare and unusual china collection. They also added heirloom antiques, art by friends, scale models, and other memorabilia.

Before they moved in their belongings, Maarten and Jetty held an open house. "It was an unveiling of our work as architects, ahead of making it into our home," Maarten says. "It was interesting how people had different but always traditional Dutch interpretations of the space. Some saw it as a barn or a church. Others saw it as a ship, or even a windmill."

Elsa de Buys, Jeroen Helsloot, Puck, and Dot, live in the center of Utrecht, a medieval city thirty miles south of Amsterdam. On the day I visit, Puck and Dot, two baby lambs, are enjoying their last moments of domestic bliss with their foster parents, before being reintroduced to life on the farm where they were born. Preparing for the separation, Elsa and Jeroen sound like parents whose teenage kids are about to go off to college—relieved and proud, but also wistful. "They grow up so fast," Elsa sighs, as we walk from the hallway into a cozy front room. As soon as she opens the kitchen door, the two lambs escape and race each other around the living room, leaping all over a red velvet sofa, into the garden and back to the kitchen where the smaller one stops to nibble at my shoelaces. "I'm sorry," Jeroen says, "but they eat everything from my socks to Elsa's linens, and all the flower buds in the garden." Puck bleats. Dot jumps straight into the air. Their race resumes and Jeroen offers to show me around the rest of the house.

It's been home for his entire life, he explains, and when his mother moved to the countryside, he and Elsa bought it from her. The house has three floors and dates back to the seventeenth century. (One of the outer walls is even older.) "My parents divorced when I was three and as man of the house, I started fixing things at an early age," he says.

When Jeroen was fifteen, he found the vestiges of the original spiral staircase that led to the third floor. He became obsessed with figuring out its dimensions and the way the wooden treads must have curved. "My mother suggested I build a model," he says and holds up a small wooden stair that sits atop the piano. "This is where it all started," he laughs. We walk to the second floor and there, in front of a large paneled window, is the staircase that he built as a boy. It looks graceful, solid and has been painted a perfect shade of eggshell blue. The Utrecht historical society praised his work, and the local paper wrote an article about him. Ever since he's been crafting staircases that are in demand all over the Netherlands, from churches, libraries, and stately homes to more contemporary projects. The most complex one he ever built was for Winkel van Sinkel, a well-known bar in the center of town. "It emulates the spiral of a seashell," he says.

The bells from a nearby church chime twelve, as we sit at the kitchen table for coffee, homemade bread, and cheese from the Hondspol farm where Elsa volunteers. The door to the garden is open and Puck and Dot are happily asleep in a cardboard box behind us. "Five years ago, a friend fostered her first newborn lamb. She told us to come over, and we were hooked as soon as we saw it," Elsa says. Jeroen smiles at the recollection and adds: "It seemed surreal to be able to have that much cuteness in your own home." Determined to have her own bottle lamb, Elsa started volunteering at the farm and they became foster parents the following spring. Lulu, their first lamb, was very weak and died almost right away. "It was sad. But then we got Mikki, and she thrived," Elsa says. By now, they've nursed nine lambs, often two at the same time. "We need one for each of us!" Jeroen laughs.

Elsa and Jeroen don't seem to mind the lambs jumping all over the furniture and racing around their carefully curated collection of vintage objects. "The advantage of living on one of the most desirable canals in Utrecht is that people throw out antiques and not Ikea," Elsa says. This way, a Murano chandelier, a walnut dresser, a Victorian chair, a piano, and a birdcage have found their way into their home. Jeroen is always on the lookout for architectural salvage to use in his work.

As I wander around the house, I discover more of their cozy and quirky gestures, from the socks on the feet of their kitchen chairs (for muffling the sound of wood scraping on stone) to a hops garland on the water fountain, a tiny toy lamb in a teacup, and a cabinet-like bathroom inspired by the classic Dutch *bedstee*—a bed in a closet.

Elsa, who has a degree in social anthropology, became more aware of her buying habits after she worked in Pakistan, and witnessed intense poverty and child labor firsthand. Now, she only buys secondhand clothing and has rekindled the craft of mending. "A beautiful repair is like creating a new layer of life," she says, as she shows me artful patches on worn-out jeans, rewoven fabric on a sofa that was attacked by the cat, repaired lace that was nibbled by lambs, and colorful embroideries on sweaters and socks. Every March, just before lambing season begins, she participates in MendMarch, an Instagram community that shares creative mending ideas and encourages a more sustainable approach to fashion. "I only ever buy what I truly love," Elsa says. "Once it's mine, I want to keep it with me for a very long time."

"I paint with fibers," says artist Claudy Jongstra, whose large-scale textiles can be found in private collections and at museums around the world, including the Cooper Hewitt, the Barnes Foundation, and SFMoMA. All of her pieces are entirely home-grown, which means that every strand of wool, and every color she uses, originates at her farm in Friesland. I visited her compound twice, once in the spring and once in late summer. Both times it was hard to wrap my head around the scale of Claudy's work and its humble, typically Dutch, origins.

On my first visit, Anna, the studio manager, takes me around the dye studio, the sheep pen, the barn where the carding takes place, and a small laboratory garden where their first dye plants were grown but that is now being turned into an aromatherapy garden. She also introduces me to "the team," a group of employees and interns as well as an elderly couple, who are live-in volunteers. "Now that we're retired, we want to give back to something meaningful," they tell me. In the afternoon, an intern named Mus shows me a Victorian greenhouse that was transplanted from a field in England, a barn with a large clay oven, a gypsy caravan where disadvantaged children attend art classes, and fields with budding calendula, chamomile, onion, and indigo that are used for coloring Claudy's textiles.

I meet Claudy on my second visit, the same day a group of art students from Groningen has come for their annual tour. She mistakes me for their teacher and seems surprised when I start to interview her. She has little time to talk, but invites me to have lunch with her crew and visitors. I photograph the compound on my own, steering clear of the swarming students. This time around, the fields are fecund, the trees are green, and instead of the silent fog that enveloped everything last spring, the sky is wide and blue and filled with swallows.

Claudy and her partner Claudia moved here from Amsterdam, where they worked from a studio near the floating flower market on the Singel canal. At that time, Claudy owned eight sheep, which she kept for the wool in her felted textiles. "I chose Drenthe Heath sheep, because they were Europe's oldest and purest breed and in danger of extinction," she says. But without her own land, she constantly had to move them from farm to farm, dike to dike, field to field, and they needed a real home. "I discovered that every square meter in this country was already being used for some kind of agriculture!" she laughs.

They looked for a property that better suited their family's lifestyle, work ethic, and growing flock of sheep and found a farm in Spannum, a tiny hamlet fifteen miles from Workum, the village where Claudy's ancestors lived more than a century ago. They soon expanded their workshops to an adjoining barn, and as their commitment to sustainable farming grew, they bought a second farm in nearby Huns. Their sons, Aebel and Jesk, attended the Waldorf School in Leeuwarden (the capital of Friesland), where Claudy and Claudia learned about Rudolf Steiner's teachings on biodynamic farming. "I recognized his ideas in what I was trying to do, without being aware of him," Claudy says, explaining how Steiner's anthroposophy (a spiritual

doctrine that integrates a connection to nature into every aspect of life) became the inspiration for the way they live on their own land.

They recently renovated the white brick house at the Huns farm, and plan to live there as soon as they find time to move. Their lives seem to extend beyond a traditional concept of home and family, as they travel all over the world to collaborate with clients, and create art while working their land communally. Even the kitchen in the Huns barn is used for family meals, public events, and baking bread for everyone, including the local community.

"Claudia's knowledge of agriculture made it possible to grow and develop all our own colors," Claudy says, "and now we understand not only the origins but also the kinetic cycles in which our crops grow." She goes on to explain how a connection to the land affects the energy of her work; how the wellbeing of her sheep, the purity of her soil, and her relationship to the people who help grow, harvest, prepare, and dye the wool, adds powerful energy to her textiles. Recently, she has introduced this energy to public spaces like the Antoni van Leeuwenhoek cancer institute in Amsterdam, where her wall hanging *Spring of Light* is meant to soothe and give emotional support.

"The colors in my work are similar to those used by the Dutch Masters," she adds, referring to Rembrandt, Vermeer, and van Gogh. "They all used natural pigments from plants that were grown in this same soil, under the same stars, and with similar weather conditions. I believe that the DNA of these colors resonates with people."

When graphic designers Petra Janssen and Edwin Vollebergh first saw the automobile repair shop in Den Bosch, it had been abandoned for thirty years. The roof had collapsed and most of the interior was in ruins, yet Petra and Edwin didn't see it that way. They only saw what it could and would be, what they now call their playground. "It was important for us to create a space where family life, creativity, and work would come together," Petra says. "We wanted it to be a mirror of our multifaceted lives."

They recycled most of the existing steel beams, restored the mezzanine level, and replaced the skylights with thermal glass. To break up the big space, they asked their friend Piet Hein Eek, a colleague from the Eindhoven Design Academy (DAE), to create a divider that would separate the studio from the living areas. It would also house their collection of vases, comic books, and other quirky ephemera. The result was a large blue wall entirely made from recycled doors and windows.

Petra takes me up to the mezzanine, and looking down, I experience a kind of creative vertigo. It's like I've entered a skylit microcosm that contains the eclectic culture of Petra and Edwin, their two sons, two cats, one dog, and Studio Boot (their design firm). "It's only an accumulation of parenting, working, and staying playful," Petra laughs.

Entertaining friends and clients is part of their creative process, and home meets work in the kitchen, over lunch and dinner. Beyond the kitchen is a large, walled-in garden, a sanctuary that used to be a graveyard for rusting cars, but now produces apples, pears, and walnuts, as well as flowers, pumpkins, leafy greens, and vegetables, in raised garden beds. There's also a sunken tub for outdoor bathing, and a long wooden table where everyone comes together in the summer.

Petra and Edwin's desks are across from each other in one of the two rooms that replicate the glass-paneled offices of the former repair shop. The second one is for employees and meetings. "Our team complements us," Edwin says. He goes on to explain how he met Petra 30 years ago at the Royal Academy of Art in Den Bosch, and how working together has strengthened their creativity. "I'm all about the details and Petra has the broader, social overview that defines our vision," he says.

One wall of the studio is lined with Edwin's posters. His unique graphics and bright, often fluorescent, colors are used for promoting causes and art, music, or theater festivals and even soccer matches. The posters have become collectable artworks, and Edwin recently discovered that counterfeit copies were being sold online. "I phoned the guy and he had the audacity to say that it was a compliment!" he says.

Petra thrives on social engagement. She taught at DAE in its heyday, when Lidewij Edelkoort was its director, and Anthon Beeke was head of the graphic design program. "We turned traditional learning on its head, Petra says. "When my time there ended, I felt the need to replace teaching with something equally challenging." An opportunity came in 2011, when Petra and Edwin staged a sustainable design festival near their hometown of Den Bosch. Again, they collaborated with Piet Hein Eek,

who created picnic tables for a temporary restaurant, using scrap wood held together by industrial straps. Amarant, a nearby workshop for people with autism, volunteered to help Piet Hein with the construction of the tables. Based on their collaboration, Petra and Amarant launched *HOUT* (Dutch for wood), a collection of furniture made from recycled lumber.

Inspired by the response to *HOUT*, Petra and her friend Simone Kramer started Social Label. With Petra's background in design and Simone's experience in public relations, they planned a labor strategy for people with poor employment prospects. "Everyone deserves a good life and if you apply inclusive design and communication on a local level, you're addressing sustainability in rewarding ways," Petra says.

After our interview at the studio, Petra takes me to the new Social Label Design Lab. It's housed in a former cattle feed plant that was donated to the organization by the city of Den Bosch. Over the past eight years, Petra, Edwin, and Simone have converted the plant into a design incubator, workspace, and retail platform.

As we walk by a giant grain silo that has been made into an office, Petra explains how Social Labor connects each designer with his or her group. "We call them the makers," she says. These men and women, who are either physically or mentally challenged, are empowered not just by the income they receive but by the sense of pride the work gives them. "So far we have produced brooms made from recycled bicycles, ceramic vases, light fixtures, clocks, aprons and other linens, tote bags, and a collection of tableware called *KOM* (bowl in Dutch) that Edwin created," she says.

Petra takes me to the other side of the silo, where several trestle tables are stacked with cups, bowls, and plates. They look like Delft crockery, but on closer inspection, I realize that the images resemble tattoos. "It's an order for *KOM* and it's going to the Cooper Hewitt Museum in New York," Petra says.

At the inception of *KOM*, Edwin asked for design input from his group of makers. It turned out that they all loved tattoos, so he created stickers that would easily transfer onto china. The makers choose their own tattoo-blue prints for every piece, with iconic images like wheelchairs with wings, ice cream cones, and hearts and slogans like "*Trots*" (Proud), "*Ik Ben Wat Ik Maak*" (I Am What I Make), and "Life Is a Bitch."

On our way out, Petra shows me a picture of the opening day of the *Werkwarenhuis* (Workwarehouse) that was held in May 2018. It shows Her Royal Highness Queen Máxima of the Netherlands sitting, smiling, between Petra and Simone. A group of men and women, young and old, surrounds the three of them. "Everyone was there, in our melting pot. Our supporters, our makers, our designers, and even our Queen," she says.

"I knew him before he knew me," says Jip, describing how, at age fifteen, she felt an instant attraction to Valentin as he whizzed by on his skateboard, along the quay of the Maas River. Fifteen years later, Valentin Loellmann and Jip Linckens live together in Maastricht, the most southern town in the Netherlands. The city was first built as a Roman fortress in the fourth century and subsequent occupations by Spain, France, and Germany have left a romantic, mystical impression on it. With its fortresses, towers, and churches, Maastricht feels more spiritual than the rest of the Netherlands, and perhaps that's why Jip's prophecy doesn't sound so strange to me. "It felt as if we were connected by an invisible thread that reached into the future," she says.

Valentin is German by birth but he attended the Maastricht Academy of Fine Arts and Design, where he was studying product design when Jip first noticed him. Three years later, Jip befriended Jonas, Valentin's younger brother, who introduced the two at a popular jazz club. "It had been a long time since that first sighting, but the feeling that we were connected was even stronger," she says.

They began seeing more of each other but shortly after their first date, fate took a cruel turn. Jip was hit by a car while riding her bicycle. She broke her back on the curb and ended up in a full body cast. "So the first months of our love affair were purely platonic," she laughs. Later, when Jip was still in a wheelchair, her father would carry her up the stairs to Valentin's apartment and place her on the sofa. She and Valentin would watch movies, drink wine, and talk into the wee hours. "Our relationship is so strong because of the spiritual bond we created during that time," Valentin says.

Eventually, they moved in together and on weekends they'd visit old houses that were for sale. "We'd fantasize about how we'd fix them up," Jip says. She'd only just graduated from art school, and Valentin was using all of his resources to establish his budding furniture studio. "We couldn't afford to buy anything, so it was more like a hobby," Valentin says. "Until we saw this place."

Their house is the last one in a row of historic workers' cottages set on the bank of the Maas River. It was the only house that hadn't been renovated. Despite its historic assignation, they were allowed to alter the interior of the house, and Valentin enlarged the rooms and plastered the remaining walls in white stucco, shaping rounded corners and edges, to create the organic look of a Mediterranean cottage. Valentin's father, a ceramicist, made tiles for the kitchen and bathrooms, and his sister created a wooden inlay floor for the hallway. Valentin fabricated almost all the furniture, except for the bathtub, which he found on *Marktplaats*, a Dutch version of eBay. The backyard is set into a hillside, a rare thing in the Netherlands, and is overgrown with bamboo.

We sit, eat cheese sandwiches, and talk on the back patio under a curtain of lilac wisteria. The soothing sound of trickling water comes from the fountain in a bright blue reflecting pool. Serene yet grounded, Jip radiates the mystical confidence

that everything is and will be okay. "Those intense early days together made it possible to give and take all the freedom we need," she says. An illustrator and author of fairytales, she's more introverted than Valentin and needs time alone to write and paint. Most days, her mother comes to the house to look after their four-year-old daughter, allowing Jip to work on her books. As they speak about their life, the couple use the words "energy" and "calm" over and over. Valentin describes their home as an oasis. He also stresses that his workdays are unconventional and that often, after coming home in the late afternoon he might return to the workshop to work late and spend the night. He speaks rapidly, changing from English to Dutch to German, as he tells me about his involvement with the Blue Mountain School in London, his upcoming solo exhibition in New York, and the restoration of a landmark building he recently bought for a new—enlarged—workshop, educational foundation, and Hortus (botanical garden).

When I visit the Valentine Loellmann studio, a former hat factory in the center of Maastricht, I experience the yin and yang quality of Valentin's life. Where his home is soothing, quiet, and feminine, his workshop is intense, noisy, and decidedly masculine. Men in visors and protective gear look like warriors as they work on large sculptural pieces, sparks flying from their welding tools. The noise from sanding and hammering metal is overwhelming. The office space, separated from the workshop by a greenhouse filled with tall plants and bamboo, is quieter. I ascend a vintage spiral staircase onto the mezzanine level where I meet Jip's father, who works as Valentin's in-house architect, as well as Jonas, Valentin's brother, who is preparing food in the open kitchen. "Lunchtime is important," Valentin says. "It's when we connect and laugh together."

We eat at a large table overlooking the backyard that's also overgrown with bamboo. There's another reflecting pool, as well as a greenhouse and sauna. When I joke that we're sitting on several hundred thousand dollars worth of his furniture, Valentin says that he prefers to use his tables and chairs as everyday functional objects. Meanwhile galleries in Paris, London, and New York display his furniture as high-value art objects. (There's a waiting list of at least six months for one of his pieces.)

Valentin describes his art as a relentless balancing of energy. He's like the alchemist who constantly adjusts ingredients—his environment, his partners, his materials, the physical, the metaphysical, and most of all nature—to create a kind of equilibrium. He speaks about nature's energy as if it were magic and influences our lives regardless of whether we're paying attention. He wants to capture this energy in the new botanical garden he's planning, and put younger generations in touch with it. "We don't create nature, we're made by nature," Valentin says, "and when we're open to it, nature can lead us anywhere."

Helma Bongenaar, Jeroen Alberts, and their children, Teun and Mies, live on a corner in Amsterdam Noord. Their house isn't far from the old harbor and, in an early incarnation, it was a kroeg—an iconic "Brown Café"—where sailors and dock workers collected and spent their wages. By the time Helma and Jeroen moved in, after graduating from art school in 1997, the interior of the kroeg was long gone and had been replaced by sheetrock walls and standard fixtures. Yet, from the moment Helma opens her door to me, I find it impossible to imagine that the interior is anything but authentic. The tall kitchen cabinets, the vintage floorboards, the ceiling with its panels and painted details, the steps and leaded glass doors that lead from the kitchen to the living room—everything feels like it has been there for hundreds of years.

Helma places a perfect mini bundt cake in front of me and gives it a dusting of powdered sugar from a vintage glass shaker. She tells me how she comes from a family of collectors, and how she has an early memory of herself sitting atop a huge pile of fabric. She was seven or eight, and Ploeg Stoffen, a Dutch weaver of specialty fabrics, was having its annual sale of "by the kilo" remnants. Her mother had gone back into the factory and left Helma with the job of protecting her loot. "We were hard core," she laughs.

Helma and Jeroen decided to recreate their home's historic past by using only salvaged materials. "Ten years ago, you could still find amazing old wood, like doors and paneling," Helma says. They'd bike around the city looking for dumpsters and whenever they found a good one, Jeroen would rush home to get the car, while Helma (once again) stayed behind to guard their discovery. They also enlisted their friends, who'd tell them when an old house was being renovated. It was through word of mouth that the two leaded glass doors were discovered in the attic of an old house around the corner.

They collaborate well, which Helma attributes to their different personalities; Jeroen is a craftsman who works with materials like wood, stone, and metal, whereas she uses fabric as well as pieces from her collections. "I like to see results right away, whereas he prefers a meticulous process," she says.

Helma gathers most of her collections at flea markets and secondhand stores. She looks for everyday stuff that's no longer popular, like the silk scarves women used to wear around their hair when riding their bicycle. She color-coordinated her scarf collection into three groups and sewed them together into sets of curtains for the kitchen and living room. When Persian rugs on tables (a Dutch tradition) became a thing of the past, vintage stores and flea markets were flooded with them. Helma bought dozens of the small rugs and sewed them together, creating one big carpet for the master bedroom.

There's something magical about the way Helma uses the repetition of small mundane items to create substantial, original pieces of furniture, like the large chandelier made from Chinese soupspoons that hangs over the kitchen table.

"A girl can never have enough chinoiserie," Helma laughs. "But I'm running out of space." There's also her collection of giant brass flies—ashtrays from France (made obsolete by the decline in smoking) that fills one wall of the living room. And, rather than a single mirror over the sink, the bathroom walls are lined with vintage hand mirrors.

Her collection of woolen blankets is an Ikea side effect, now that everyone has switched to comforters. "I love old woolen blankets that are scratchy, pilly, and felted from too much washing," Helma says. She especially likes the logos that depict cozy Dutch scenes of kittens and lambs and has combined the labels into one stunning quilt. She also turned her blankets into poufs that are used as footstools in front of the sofa. "I cut my blankets into circles because fabric frays less that way and sew them on top of one another," she says.

Food makes up another part of Helma's life. Her mother was a chef who taught French cooking classes and welcomed everyone at her table. "She taught me a love for food and hospitality, but never how to cook," Helma says. She has continued her mother's tradition in her own kitchen, and several times a year she prepares a five-course feast for paying guests. "It started with this fun Facebook event called Restaurant Day," she explains. "Amateur chefs would host dinners and post them live, starting with New Zealand. The dinners would move around the world, and by the time we were done eating, New York would get started." From making the house perfect to shopping, cooking, setting the table, and cleaning up, it takes Helma three days to organize and execute each event. "It's really more like a performance piece," she laughs.

Helma's good taste is reflected by her first cookbook, *Au Bon Coin*, where Dutch and French cooking is shown against the background of her life. The (Dutch) recipes all start with the letter A; from Ardeche to Amsterdam, Asparagus to Avocado, and Almond to Aperitif.

The magazine *Sentimental Journal*, which Helma co-founded with her friend Linda Loenen, is a visual expression of the meaning Helma finds in cultural icons of the past as well as the present. "It doesn't have to be old," she says, "but the passion of each maker needs to shine, be it in an object, a photograph, or a life well lived."

In 2017, interior and product designer Tjimkje de Boer bought a seven-thousand-square-foot former ammunitions warehouse. The building borders on a small, man-made forest, named *Het Blofbos* (the blast forest) by the locals, that was created as a sound buffer for test explosions between the secret Hembrug arms factory and the nearby village of Zaandam. A short ferry ride from Amsterdam, the former arsenal sits on a hundred-acre peninsula surrounded by canals that feed into the IJ harbor. After years of repurposing studies, Hembrug was recently opened up for redevelopment, and now, a decade later, stern no-trespassing signs remain dotted throughout the refurbished streets, as reminders of its ominous legacy. As I drive by the Yada Yada food court, the stark contrast between the creative environment of galleries, ateliers, lofts, and cool-looking people and the manufacture of weapons of mass destruction, feels ironic.

The day of my visit coincides with Open House at Artzaanstad, a museum of contemporary art. As Tjimkje and I sit at her picnic table, shaded by century-old elm trees, drinking tea and talking, we are interrupted by lost art lovers, who are either searching for the museum or the way home. Tjimkje patiently explains that the ferry is the fastest way back to Amsterdam. One couple stops to see if this is a restaurant and another group, dressed like the Addams family, wants to look inside. They act offended when Tjimkje clarifies that her studio is private.

I ask her how she feels about Hembrug's transition from artillery to art. She answers that its dark past doesn't really bother her. "If anything, we were lucky!" she says. "Where else can you still get a huge space like this?"

Tjimkje speaks in the plural but when I ask about a partner, she laughs. "You can replace we with me. I pretty much do it all myself." After being abandoned for years, the warehouse was a wreck. She began the restoration process by pouring new concrete floors and replacing the rotting wooden boards with recycled rafters and planks. The roof also needed repairs but the glass windowpanes were surprisingly intact. She built partitions, as well as two bathrooms and a kitchen. The original doors had been removed and left in neat stacks on the second floor. She sanded and repainted them in their authentic green color, before matching them back into their original frames.

Despite turning a downstairs space into a workshop for her furniture design, Tjimkje found it hard to develop new products while she was in the midst of construction. "Now, I'm finally creative again," she says, "and working on new acoustic designs as well as furniture." She is perfecting the sound-dampening light fixtures that she developed with engineer Michiel Post, her partner in Acoustic Design Solutions who is also a tenant in the building. "It's great to have him here, so we can experiment together," she says and explains how she designs the lamps based on Michiel's sound research and data.

Perhaps influenced by her paradoxical environment, Tjimkje appears restless while in search of stillness. Her work is often ironic. She intentionally left the layers of flaking plaster and paint throughout her studio yet uses playful modern gestures in the design of her furniture, including a chair design that looks like two oversized wooden buttons sewn together by black (steel) rope. During her extensive travels, she photographs things that only later come into focus in the execution of her products. Her pictures of Eastern rice paddies inspired the layered design of her acoustic lamp, and the colorful shadows cast by the leaded glass windows inside an Italian church inspired the oxidized glass for her mirrors and tabletops.

Upstairs, Tjimkje has created her own private sanctuary away from the raw industrial workspaces of the first floor. For the walls she combined colors that are inspired by her travels to Colombia and Bolivia, while creating contrast by painting a black and white "rug," reminiscent of midcentury geometric art, on the wooden floor.

Her passion for kitesurfing explains the wetsuit that hangs on a room divider made from three recycled doors. Next to it hangs a gold-sequined sexy dress. "I use the wetsuit, but I've never worn the dress," she says wistfully. "I got it in Spain. It felt so right on me, but when I came back here I realized there aren't many Dutch events that are glitzy enough for a gown like this!"

Liesbeth and Marco van Houselt found their house thirty years ago, as they were searching for a fixer-upper farm. It had been Marco's dream to renovate old houses ever since he was a boy, and the sale of their former home, in an affluent suburb south of Amsterdam, meant that he could afford to make his dream come true. They explored the Dutch countryside, still relatively undiscovered thirty years ago, and settled on the Betuwe, which means "good land" in old Germanic and describes the extremely fertile soil between three of the country's largest rivers: the Lek, the Waal, and the Meusse. It's also called the orchard of the Netherlands.

Their farm sits a few feet below the water level of the Waal River, behind a high dike that stops the land from flooding. The previous occupants were dairy farmers whose living quarters were in the front of the farm, while the cow stables were in the rear, connected by a door in the mudroom. The living area was designed for warmth and practicality. The ceilings were dropped, the original doors hidden by newer wooden panels, and the hearth had one gas heater that was meant to warm the entire home. The bedrooms were cold and tiny and the kitchen had last been updated in the 1950s with Formica counters and plywood cabinets. They gutted the house in stages and did all the renovation work themselves with the help of both their fathers. Liesbeth's mother would bring along casseroles, cakes, and cookies and entertained her grandsons, who were toddlers at the time, while everyone else worked on the house. The couple looks back on those five years of renovation with fondness. "We never took a holiday," Marco says, "but being creative together was fun and *gezellig*."

They both feel that reclaiming an old house is addictive yet they never had the urge to sell up and start over. "Once you're finished at one end, there's always stuff to do at the other," Marco laughs. A businessman, he worked long hours, and Liesbeth was a stay-at-home mother. In hindsight she realizes that she remained creative by making clothes, drawing with her boys, and creating the sets and costumes for their school plays. "She can make anything," Marco says proudly.

After her sons had left for college, Liesbeth went through a dark, melancholy phase of her life that she only managed to leave behind when she discovered art therapy. "When I began painting, everything fell into place," she says. "I always knew I was creative, but I didn't know my life depended on it."

When I first saw Liesbeth and Marco's house in a Dutch lifestyle magazine, her bold paintings stood out, but the photo stylist had given the home a French brocante character—vintage cute with flowers and lace and dainty details. It turns out that Liesbeth's style is more soulful, and her paintings, robust and often rendered on corroded surfaces, tell more about her spirit than the white bouquets and doilies of those photos.

Liesbeth has been painting for eleven years now. As a child she staged still lifes in her room, using her toys and trinkets. Later she did the same around the house, intuitively arranging her things like pictures. Her early paintings are

renderings of her arrangements like glass bottles in a crate, saddlebags in the hallway, blue blankets on a chair, and a row of typical Dutch clogs, all paintings that are scattered around the house, often as part of a larger, coordinated tableau.

Four times a week, Liesbeth teaches a painting course. She started these classes to cover the cost of the new art barn they'd built to replace several derelict outbuildings. It's a simple structure of about fifteen hundred square feet, with an equally large loft that is filled with Liesbeth's experiments on sheets of corroded steel, burlap potato sacks, lengths of indigo dyed linen, and starched canvas embossed with patterns.

She paints and lectures on the main floor, which smells of turpentine. Light filters in through dusty windows and long tables filled with brushes in glass jars stand in the middle of the space. A row of easels lines the wall and one corner is stacked with blank canvases. Partially finished paintings sit between props like vases, chairs, and stacks of books and fabrics. A portrait of a boy peeks through the spokes of an old chair, a still life of newspapers sits next to a pile of real newspapers, and an oval palette with dried paint leans against a bluestone sink.

Her students are mainly older women; some are seasoned artists and others are newcomers. All of them paint for the same reason, something that she recognizes from her own experience. "It's meditation," Liesbeth says, "a way to get in touch with yourself." She wishes there were a few younger women in her class, but admits that women are generally too busy and preoccupied to take time for themselves. Some of her pupils come to get away from stressful jobs and others wait until their children have left and their careers become less prominent.

The rest of the week she spends by herself in the studio or in nature around the house, painting in the fields, orchards, and along the river. She admits that she's a bit of a hermit, and that she's content working in solitude. "I sometimes regret that I didn't know this about myself sooner," she says, smiling. "But I'm happy with the life I have."

Rolf Bruggink's place is like *The Secret Garden*. Hidden behind a tall brick wall that's overgrown with ivy, it feels as if he intentionally makes it hard to find a way in. Even on my second visit, I roam around for ten minutes, knocking on several large, forbidding doors, before I hear him holler: "HERE!" Like I should've known all along.

The property sits just off the Maliebaan, a Dutch landmark with a long, diverse history. It was first developed in 1640 as the field where Utrecht's gentry played *Malie*, a popular game somewhere between golf and croquet. When the game went out of fashion, the land was converted to livestock grazing. During the Second World War, several of the old mansions that bordered on the field became the headquarters of the NSB, the Dutch political party of German sympathizers.

Rolf's compound is located behind the mansions, at the end of a mews lined with nineteenth-century workers' cottages. He and Yffi, his partner of twenty-eight years, initially bought the coach house, a handsome brick building of about 1,100 square feet with a high ceiling, tall windows on one side, and doors big enough for horse-drawn carriages. When the local council slated the adjoining barrack for demolition, they decided to buy it. Now, six years later, three garden studios are hidden behind the old brick walls and blackened fences.

"Initially, I designed a sculptural insertion that left the integrity of the coach house untouched," Rolf explains. He seems restless and reluctant to dwell in the past and starts telling me about the home he's currently building in Senegal.

During his career as an architect, Rolf specialized in turning old churches and watermills into high-end residences, and when he bought the Maliebaan property, he knew exactly what he wanted. He enlisted the help of Niek Wagemans, a reuse specialist, when it became clear just how much material the barrack would yield. Rolf explains how the collaboration with Niek was invaluable as they reworked all the salvage into the interior of the coach house.

The demolished barrack was about thirty by sixty feet, with practical, mid-century, construction. The walls were made of glass, and below the windows ran 160 feet of radiators. The roof consisted of wooden beams and boards, most of them in good condition. After bleaching and sanding the salvaged roofing lumber, Rolf and Niek used it throughout the insertion, sideways or flat, horizontal as well as vertical, creating different textures for the walls and two staircases. The leftover tar-stained wood made for a powerful blackened wall in the kitchen. The window panels were left intact to create a partition that separates the kitchen from the living area. "It was our intention to use up every single piece of material," Rolf says. For the outer wall of the sculptural insertion, they used the old radiators, creating a self-supporting system. "Fusing them like building blocks was more interesting than just tacking them to a wooden framework," he says. They hid the old gypsum panels inside the walls, as insulation, but the aluminum suspension system became another design texture, used for the wall of the main stairwell. "And this table is our sample card,"

Rolf says, tapping its leg. "You can see the leftovers of every material that went into the building."

When he turned fifty, Rolf took a year off for reflection. "I was spending too much time in design meetings," he says of the architecture practice he left behind. "I realized my happiness depended on being more autonomous." After moving in to the new space, he went on to do more sculptural product design, using mostly discarded materials.

In 2004, in the aftermath of the Indian Ocean tsunami, Rolf, Yffi, and several of their friends went to assist the affected communities in Sri Lanka. Since then, the group raises money and uses it for development projects such as building schools, orphanages, and septic systems in places like India, Cambodia, Haiti, and Tanzania. "We pay our own way, so all the money goes into these projects," Rolf says.

Most recently they worked in Senegal, and, in the process of renovating several schools, the couple fell in love with the country and its people. "We'd been looking for a place to escape the dreary Dutch winters," he says, "so we bought some land and are building a small house."

A few months later, I check in with Rolf to see if he made it back to Senegal. He tells me that the pandemic has affected his plans. With all travel to Africa on hold, he's been working on a water tower conversion near Rotterdam, spending time in his house in France, and sketching out ideas for, what he calls, an architectural vacation community.

"This keeping-distance culture isn't so bad for introverts," he says. "Yffi and I have discovered that we're both introverts!"

A rusty wall that resembles a giant railroad track appears to run through Jeroen and Laura van Zwetselaar's rescued station house in Santpoort, as if they want to ground their home (and life) to the site forever. "Yes, maybe," Jeroen says, when I share this thought. "But tracks also signify movement."

He tells me how he lives his life in intense cycles that begin with a period of cocooning. When he emerges from the "chrysalis" he first needs to feel grounded before starting new ventures.

The latest cycle began when he bought the derelict station. As a successful creative director he'd lost himself in the process of designing new identities for products, spaces, and people. Even though he tried to be green, inclusive, and sustainable with each campaign, he disliked the misleading nature of commercial marketing. He sold the company to his partner, separated from his first wife, and moved into the shed that sat on the edge of the overgrown railroad property. "I intentionally made my life very small," he says.

Like a male version of *Sleeping Beauty*, he stirred from this dormant state when Laura came along. She was an executive in the fashion business and admits that she wasn't used to free-spirited entrepreneurs. "I didn't know what to make of his life in a ruined station," she says, "but he was a beautiful human being and somehow I trusted his creative process."

For the next three years, Jeroen worked on transforming the delapidated station into a home for Laura, Saam, the son from his first marriage, and himself. He tore out all the walls, restored the old house, and created additional space by adding the steel clad structure. The "grounded" phase of their life started when they finally moved from the shed to the house. "Raaf and Ramses were both born here, which created even more of an anchor for us," Laura says.

As he worked on the house, Jeroen further developed his identity as an interior designer. "In the process I came home to myself," he says. Watching Jeroen evolve inspired Laura to take risks of her own. She left the fashion business and began working with him. "When I was pregnant it made sense to merge everything together," she says. They'd reached a certain place in life, and all they wanted now was comfort. "Not luxury," Jeroen stresses, "but a balance between family, work, and our responsibility to the world around us."

Laura is good with people and helps translate Jeroen's talent and vision into successful collaborations with their employees and clients. "Happy employees make happy work," she says. They apply a similar approach to their clients by creating environments that leave everyone happy. "The interiors should never be about me," Jeroen says, "but about the spirit of the original space and the people who live there."

Their studio, ZW6, specializes in converting old farm buildings, cottages, canal houses, and former industrial sites. Jeroen's style is casual, almost nonchalant. He creates new spaces that feel like they've been lived in for years, reflecting the heritage of the original structure. He brings in light and nature by installing large

windows and opening up rooms by removing walls. He exposes old beams, bricks and floors and leaves them as they are. Then, he introduces other elements, sometimes using salvaged materials or adding new textures like steel, glass, marble, and concrete. He applies textiles in muted colors to add a layer of warmth. It's exactly this balance of old and new, and soft and solid that gives his work the feeling of homey, weathered luxury.

With a growing family and expanding client base, the ZW6 studio outgrew the railroad property and Jeroen bought and renovated another old building in nearby Bloemendaal. "It was a rabbit warren of little offices within the confines of an old factory," he says. He stripped the existing interior down to rafters and brick walls and poured a concrete floor. The fifteen hundred square feet of empty space was like a blank canvas for vignettes of his work, with a model living room, kitchen, bedroom, and bathroom. Wood and steel workstations are scattered throughout the displays and match the interior designs in a way that renders them almost invisible. This casual mix of office and residential showroom also makes for a cozy work environment. There's even a piano, and after school the three boys hang out in the model kitchen, eating peanut butter sandwiches while Saam does his homework at the sample dining table. "Often a client buys the sample from the showroom, and the empty space this creates is an opportunity to come up with a new design," Jeroen says.

Even during the Covid-19 lockdown ZW6 stayed busy. "People seem more focused on nesting now, than before," Laura says. Sometimes they saw their clients on Zoom, but they also met for design meetings at the studio, which is large enough for everyone to stay socially distanced. She admits that having three boisterous boys at home full-time was a bigger challenge. Looking for a solution, she met with Saam's mother, and together they devised a fifty-fifty schedule for the care of their boys. "This way she and I alternated working and caretaking, and our five kids were always together as one happy family," Laura says.

Lia Harmsen built herself a tiny house in the woods near Ommen, just because it made sense. She'd been looking for a place to live and work that was small, green, and sustainable. A dedicated stonemason and sculptor, she fantasized about an art studio in nature, but each house she saw was designed for suburban families and not solitary artists. Disheartened, she looked into prefab homes and realized that, with a bit of luck and imagination, she might be able to create her dream home from scratch.

"As I searched for land online, I came across a dismal picture of a property," she says, "I grew up not far from here, so I knew the natural beauty of the area." She bought the quarter-acre lot and contacted an established prefab firm. They introduced her to Daniel Venneman, the young architect who ended up creating the entire house. Daniel and his firm, Woonpioneers, had been developing plans for a tiny home named Indigo: a system where the customer determines the size and layout of their home by putting together prefabricated building blocks.

Lia's wishes were simple: she needed a sculpture studio, a shower/toilet, a kitchen nook, and a living/bedroom. Most of all she wanted windows large enough to bring in the surrounding forest. What she got was so much more than a prefab box. The treads of the staircase are designed to double as drawers. A spacious shower is tucked beneath the stairs, and the wire railing allows for an uninterrupted view of the trees. Best of all, the vaulted ceiling reminds her of a medieval chapel, her favorite form of architecture. "And the birds like it as much as I do," she says. Attracted to the wooden siding, they started pecking holes to build their nests. Lia tried hanging mirrors from the rafters, and they moved away. "I guess they don't like to look at themselves," she laughs.

Lia teaches art, part time, at a school for children with learning disabilities in Amsterdam and divides her time equally between the city and her sculpting studio. When I spoke to her, she'd just resumed her job, after five months in Covid-19 lockdown. "I felt like royalty escaping to the countryside," she says, "but the kids and I are happy to be back together."

Both careers started after she graduated from the Zwolle art academy. Initially, she supported her sculpting studio by teaching art, but this changed after a bike trip to Spain, when she explored roadside chapels and became fascinated by gothic edifices. On her return she enrolled in a stone-working class and became an apprentice to a mason, which led to a job at an artisanal stone yard. Here, she combined her experience as an artist with the more traditional craft of masonry, creating architectural details as well as artful headstones.

Lia enjoys the balance of education and sculpting; one requires intense interaction and the other is all about solitude. "But they both work with resistance," she says, wondering if that makes sense to me. "Rocks as well as kids are full of untapped potential, and I've become good at extracting it."

To her surprise the Indigo house has been published worldwide. The architect, too, is pleased with the positive response, but is often taken aback by people

who ask for a home that is exactly like Lia's, yet ten times bigger. While this can be done, Daniel is more interested in developing large-scale projects for co-housing. "More and more people realize how many aspects of life can be shared," Lia explains. This doesn't mean they dream of living in utopian communes. Rather, they want to be part of collectives that are based on need and not greed. Daniel's plan for these types of sustainable communities focuses on reducing costs and environmental footprints, sharing practical functions, and using green technology.

Lia is bemused by the idea of communal living. "I don't even need a pet," she says. Explaining how during the recent months of quarantine, the deer, porcupines, birds, and even wolves came closer to her house than ever before, as if they sensed a change in human behavior. "Nature really doesn't need our help," she says. "In fact it's better off without us."

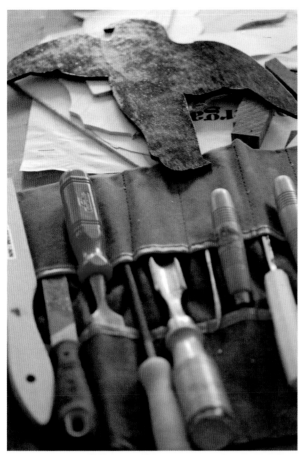

Kiki van Eijk and Joost van Bleiswijk live in an old dairy farm on the outskirts of Eindhoven, a few miles from Nuenen, the village where Vincent van Gogh lived and created his famous pre-expressionist painting *The Potato Eaters*. Joost likes to imagine Vincent passing by their farm on his exploratory walks around the countryside. "His painting called *The Poplars* looks exactly like the landscape around here," he says.

In 1891, six years after van Gogh moved away, Eindhoven attracted a new set of luminaries: the Phillips family and their electric bulb factory. The Phillips's simple mission to bring electric light into every Dutch home created one of the most successful electronics companies of the twentieth century. Whatever is in the local potatoes, it continues to inspire innovation more than a century later, as Eindhoven has become the center of Dutch design and hosts the annual Dutch Design Week, attracting tens of thousands of international visitors from around the world.

Kiki and Joost are at the core of this design movement. They attended the Eindhoven Design Academy (DAE), a world-famous interdisciplinary institute that sprang up in several of Phillips's former factory buildings. Whereas other students moved on to design jobs in Milan, Paris, and New York, the couple stayed in Eindhoven, joined a local anti-squat compound, and started making objects in an empty warehouse that became the new design lab for a group of DAE alums. "We were the pioneers," Joost says, "independent, experimental, wild, and super productive."

I help set the outdoor table for lunch and we sit down underneath vines that are heavy with bunches of grapes, grown from Joost's father's cultivars. The arbor stretches the length of a table that's long enough for sixteen guests. We sit in Jaime Hayon chairs, eat from painted china plates, and use sleek steel cutlery, the latter two designed by Kiki. Joost baked the bread and six-year-old Puk boasts that he built the pizza oven as he waves his ax around, ready to chop wood for the fire. "It's pizza night," he roars.

Kiki explains how she got her first break when sculptor Stephan Weiss, Donna Karan's husband, showed her work in an exhibition at Urban Zen, the couple's New York conceptual gallery space in the West Village. At the same time Joost, Kiki, and other Eindhoven designers were working on small collections of their own for the 2004 Milan Design Week. "It was an all or nothing start," Joost says of the prototypes they took to the *Tutto Bene* exhibition. They returned to Milan in 2005 and over the next couple of years the Dutch group made everything from ceramics to wooden furniture. For Milan Design Week 2006, Kiki and Joost were given a solo show. "That year was the birth of 'Dutch Design' with Middle Eastern sheiks buying limited edition pieces for a small fortune," Kiki says. But after the 2008 financial crash, the designer market changed. "The money just evaporated," Joost says, "but the advantage was that we'd never sold out to a gallery or brand." This meant that they could stay true to themselves, creating autonomous objects that were sold by tastemakers like Murray Moss and Moooi.

Puk returns from chopping wood to interrupt our interview. He's spotted my camera and would like to take pictures of us. "Why don't you use your Legos to make your own camera," Joost says, gently steering him toward a creative solution.

In 2013, the couple drove past the ruin of an old dairy farm just outside Eindhoven. There were "No Trespassing" signs posted all around. They fell in love with the rural location, on the edge of the city. "We were living in a small townhouse and really missed nature," Kiki says. With only an old, faded sign to go by, Joost began making calls as soon as he got home. A few weeks later, they bought the derelict property. "Our friends thought we were crazy," Kiki says, "and of course there was a certain amount of denial, considering that I was pregnant and the whole thing had to be built in less than eight months." Joost explains that the only part they didn't tear down was the perimeter wall. Everything else, the roof, floors, beams, and rafters had to be replaced. "But in the moment we never saw what it was like. We saw what it would become," he says.

Unlike other creative couples, they chose not to incorporate their studio into the new home. Instead, they share a large workshop, ten minutes away by bicycle. Sometimes they collaborate on projects but mostly they create their own collections. Kiki's playful work ranges from colorful rugs and wall hangings, to ceramic tableware and quirky furniture, while Joost makes bold, powerful furniture and light fixtures in steel, stone, and wood.

They may not work there, but the home still feels like a design lab. "It's the showroom of our life," Kiki says, explaining how all the pieces are interwoven with stories of their own, such as the prototype of Kiki's "Matrice" lamp that was bought by Karl Lagerfeld, or Joost's "Tinkering" light fixture that hangs over the dining table, which is sold by Moooi, and the 1950s-inspired upholstery fabric they created for Bernhardt Design. Other pieces connect them to their friends, like paintings by Marc Mulders, a lamp by Maarten Baas, and two identical jugs by Cor Unum that are stenciled with the names of their boys: Puk and Ko.

When I contacted the couple after the lockdown, Kiki wrote: "Actually, we've never had time for a real break, like a kind of sabbatical. Of course Covid is far from a blessing, but it has opened up new possibilities. As creators, designers, artists, we have it in us to come up with solutions. This has been a time to rethink and be flexible. In a way we've always lived like this, but now it's under a magnifying glass. This is reflected in our new work, which originated in the intimate home atmosphere during isolation and now manifests itself more freely than ever. We feel grateful for what we have."

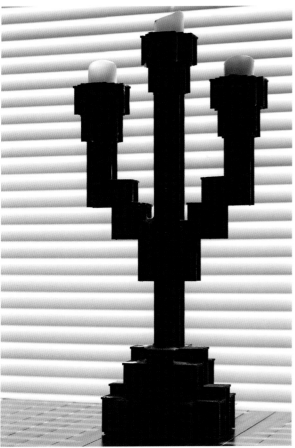

ACKNOWLEDGMENTS

Coming Home wouldn't have happened if it weren't for a confluence of people and experiences that I never saw coming. First, my twin daughters, Kiki and Leila, were curious about studying in the Netherlands and we traveled around the country to visit colleges. Next, my mother Bieneke, my sister Rebecca, and my cousins Karin and Rieteke promised to look out for Kiki and Leila if they moved. I felt as if I was returning home after a long absence. Making a book was also the perfect excuse to spend more time with my family in Amsterdam. And in the end it was the creative brilliance and support of the people featured here that took the book from a fantasy to a labor of love: Matt and Ina, Laura and John, Jetty and Maarten, Elsa and Jeroen, Claudy and Claudia, Petra and Edwin, Valentin and Jip, Helma and Jeroen, Tjimkje, Liesbeth and Marco, Rolf and Yffi, Laura and Jeroen, Lia, and Kiki and Joost. Without their inspiration, *Coming Home* would not have been possible, and I thank them from the bottom of my heart. I mustered the confidence to make my own book because Alastair, my husband and partner of thirty years, has shown me how to make beautiful publications and over time brought out my inner writer, leading me from the world of fashion to the world of publishing. Lidewij has been a mentor since the day I met her on a fashion shoot for a Dutch department store. I was an eighteen-year-old model, and she was the stylist who told me to look after my clothes as if they were my best friends. We've been best friends ever since. A book is merely a dream without a publisher and I am beyond grateful to publisher Charles Miers and editor Daniel Melamud at Rizzoli for "going Dutch" with me. I continue to learn so much from them and *Coming Home* has been our most creative collaboration so far. I am honored by the supportive words of iconic writers Wendy Goodman and Pilar Viladas as well as creative director Yolanda Edwards. I thank my four beautiful and talented children: Leila for being my photography assistant; Kiki for her graphic design work and creating the embroidered font; and Iona and Iain for their fresh eye and positive feedback. Along the long path of my life there have been the friends, mentors, and family members who helped me become who I am, and I am blessed to have had them in my life: Gail and Murray Bruce, J Morgan Puett, Solange Khavkine, Nina Burleigh, Annette Bonnier, Will Simmons, Michael Mundy, Sean Strub, Pete and Marsha Comstock, Ed and Vicki Kleban, Jayne Harkness, Calvin Klein, Jessica Velmans, Vera Graaf, Ashtiana, Susan Johnson, Vanessa Downing, Robert Barber, Caroline Goodall, Michael Hayes, Ronnie and Clare Stirling, Harry Wich, Dorien de Vos, Petra Laseur, Joyce Roodnat, Jowan van Heyningen, Cor Mieras, Opa and Oma, and of course my brother, Axel. And last but not least, I dedicate this book to my father, Jo de Vries. You left us too soon but you've been my angel ever since.

ABOUT THE AUTHOR

Barbara de Vries was born in Amsterdam. She studied fashion design in London and moved to New York in the 1990s where she created the CK collections at Calvin Klein. Subsequently, she had her own collections in the US and Japan. Barbara and her husband, Alastair Gordon, are the founders of Gordon de Vries Studio, an imprint that publishes illustrated books on design and lifestyle. She is also a passionate anti plastic pollution activist. When her twin daughters moved to the Netherlands to study design, Barbara was inspired to make a book that felt like coming home.

PHOTOGRAPHY CREDITS

Principal photographer: Barbara de Vries
Page 14, upper right: Erik Freeland
Page 15, upper right: Gilles de Chabaneix
Page 15, lower left: Bieneke Roelofs
Page 57: Sjaak Henselmans, Courtesy of Min2
Page 66: Caroline Coehorst
Page 74: Elsa de Buys
Page 91: lower left: copyright @ Claudy Jongstra
Page 95: Jean-Marc Wullschleger, courtesy of Studio Boot
Pages 112, 114, 116, 119, 120, 122.123, 124,125, 128: Jonas Loellman
Page 135: Helma Bongenaar
Pages 178, 180, 183, 184: Christel Derksen en Rolf Bruggink, courtesy of Studio Rolf
Page 204: JR works, courtesy of Studio Jeroen van Zwetselaar
Page 218: Henny van Belkom, courtesy of Woonpioneers

ART IN HOMES

Pages 4, 10: Alastair Gordon
Page 7: Klaas Gubbels
Page 25: Katinka Lampe
Page 26: Kristof Kintera
Page 33: Ina Meijer
Pages 58, 60, 61, 63 upper left: Jaap Min
Page 55: Antonie Sas
Pages 106, 108: Edwin van Vollebergh
Pages 160, 166, 172: Liesbeth van Houselt
Page 193: Erwin Olaf
Page 196: Selwyn Senatori
Page 200: Geert Kollau
Page 202: Billy und Hells
Page 220: Sabine Pigalle
Page 235: Kiki van Eijk

First published in the United States of America in 2021 by
Rizzoli International Publications, Inc.
300 Park Avenue South
New York, NY 10010
www.rizzoliusa.com

Coming Home: Modern Rustic, Creative Living in Dutch Interiors
© Barbara de Vries

Instagram/Goingdutchinteriors

Text © Barbara de Vries
Foreword © Lidewij Edelkoort
Photography and design: Barbara de Vries
Graphic design: Kiki Gordon
Editor: Alastair Gordon

For Rizzoli International Publications:
Publisher: Charles Miers
Editor: Daniel Melamud
Production: Colin Hough Trapp
Proofreader: Megan Conway

ISBN: 978-0-8478-6990-9
Library of Congress Control Number: 2021931119

Printed in China

Visit us online:
Facebook.com/RizzoliNewYork
Twitter: @Rizzoli_Books
Instagram.com/RizzoliBooks
Pinterest.com/RizzoliBooks
Youtube.com/user/RizzoliNY